SIX FIGURE
CAREER
COACHING
ADVICE

PATRICIA DORCH

THE ULTIMATE GUIDE
TO ACHIEVING SUCCESS

This publication contains the opinions, and ideas and recommendations of its author. The author and the publisher disclaim any responsibility for any liability, loss, or risk, personal, professional or otherwise, which is incurred as a consequence, directly or indirectly, of the use and application of any of the contents of this book. The strategies outlined in this book may not be suitable for every individual, and are not guaranteed or warranted to produce particular results.

Dorch, Patricia.

Six Figure Career Coaching Advice: The Ultimate Guide To Achieving Success / Patricia Dorch.

For information about special discounts for bulk purchases please contact Patricia Dorch at: www.sixfigurecareercoach.com

Email: patricia@sixfigurecareercoach.com

Printed in the United States of America

ISBN-13: 978-0-9816854-2-7

Dedication

To Willie Mae Dorch, my mother. Your love, support, encouragement to "never give up" provided me with the focus I needed to pursue my goals and purpose. Thank you for encouraging me to use the skills I have to make a positive difference in the lives of those who read my book.

To Raymond McKelvin. Thank you for your love and support, which helped me, accomplish my life's purpose. Your commitment to my goals is a reminder when you have the "will" never let your status or circumstance discourage you from achieving your goals, but pursue it with everything you have.

To Francine Dorch, my sister. Thank you for your love, support and confidence that I would accomplish my goals. Knowing you were there to help me was a comfort when I faced challenges along the way. You never told me to give up, instead you helped me and let me know you loved me and would be there when I needed you.

I want to extend my personal and sincere thanks to all who have dedicated their time, expertise and advice for this book. Their knowledge and support have contributed to my success.

Contents

Six Figure Career Coaching Advice: The Ultimate Guide To Achieving Success

Introduction

Have you ever been passed over for a promotion – and someone less qualified got the job? Do power lunches and meetings make you wonder if you're making the right impression? Would you like to improve your people skills and professional image?

As a career coach, Patricia Dorch helps her clients make changes in their professional image and learn business etiquette that allows them to advance their careers. At the same time, her advice leads them to strategically plan their future and seek networking, training and personal development opportunities that can help them build that future.

Six Figure Career Coaching Advice: The Ultimate Guide to Achieving Success contains some of Patricia's most powerful advice- and most of it is easy to start doing right away! From recent college graduates to seasoned professionals, every reader will find valuable tips and strategies they can effectively utilize.

Patricia's unique blend of experience, as both a consultant to companies and a personal career coach to employees, make her advice an invaluable guide to thriving in today's job market, getting a promotion, or improving your current career. It's all here in Six Figure Career Coaching Advice!

Power Interview Image

Planning your interview wardrobe is essential in conveying to the hiring manager that you are serious about your career. Every employee should have a quality "interview suit" reserved in his or her wardrobe for interviews. A navy blue, tailored suit makes a powerful first impression. Add a business blouse for women and a shirt and tie for men to "show you mean business" in the eyes of the hiring committee.

Although women's pant suits are widely accepted in the workplace, a "skirt suit" is more favorable during the interview process. Once you have achieved your new career, a pant suit (if appropriate for the work environment) adds an alternative business or business casual look.

During multiple interviews, be consistent in your appearance; wear suits, not separates or coordinates. Your attention to detail in the final interview phase is crucial to your success. Close the interview with your ability to perform the job. Once hired, project the same professional image you presented during your interview by dressing for your next position.

Men

Suit

- Solid dark color
- Matching jacket and trousers
- Trousers cuffed

Shirt

- Modified spread collar
- White
- Long-sleeved

Tie

- Solid, stripes or small patterns
- Conservative
- No red

Shoes

- Lace-ups only
- Dark color
- Polished and in good condition

Socks

- Dark color
- Match to trousers or shoes
- Mid-calf

Belt

- Match to trousers or shoes
- No braces (suspenders)

Jewelry

- Earrings - not recommended
- Bracelets - not recommended

Hair

- Cut and styled
- Facial hair trimmed and groomed

Fragrance

- No cologne or scented aftershave

Nail Care

- Manicured
- Neatly trimmed
- Clear polish (optional)

Attaché Case (Optional)

- Leather
- Dark color – preferably black
- Stylish
- Not oversized

Business Tools

- Leather writing tablet – dark color
- Quality ink pen
- Your personal business card
- Cell phone or pager – TURN OFF or leave in your vehicle
-

Women

Suit

- Conservative
- Solid color
- Skirt suit – recommended
- No red or fashion colors

Blouse

- Solid or small print or stripe
- No turtlenecks

Shoes

- Classic leather pumps
- Closed-toe
- Dark color
- Polished and in good condition

Jewelry

- No ankle bracelets

Hair

- Professionally styled
- No fashion hair colors

Hose

- Coordinated with attire
- No bare legs

Makeup

- Conservative application

Fragrance

- None

Nail Care

- Manicure or acrylic fill – no chipped nail polish
- No fashion bright colors or studs
- No long nails

Attaché Case (Optional)

- Leather
- Dark color – preferably black
- Stylish
- Not oversized

Business Tools

- Leather writing tablet – dark color
- Quality ink pen
- Your personal business card
- Cell phone or pager – TURN OFF or leave in your vehicle

Casual Looks for Men and Women

What Not to Wear

There are many definitions and opinions regarding what types of attire fall in the category of business casual. When in doubt, dress up a notch on the conservative side rather than the casual side, or ask your company representative. Listed are general guidelines for attire, accessories, and styles that are not considered business casual.

Athletic wear, athletic shoes, denim (jeans and jean shirts of any color), sweatshirts, sweatpants, exposed midriffs, leather wear, skorts / shorts / bermuda shorts, capri pants, uncovered sleeveless clothing, tee shirts, tanks, or tube tops, spaghetti straps and/or sun dresses, leggings and/or spandex pants, exposed cleavage, sheer clothing, short-sleeved shirts, bandanas, hats, ankle bracelets, fashion hair colors, baggy or oversized and undersized clothing, untucked shirts, military camouflage looks, swimwear, loungewear, nightwear looks, flannel pajamas, bare legs, moccasins, mid-calf strappy sandals, clogs, any color flip flops, visible body art, tattoos and piercings

Body art, tattoos and piercing are no longer reserved for bikers and sailors. These forms of non-religious "self-expression" statements have made their way to the boardroom and general population of organizations. However, self-expression statements can cross the business line and form unfavorable perceptions about your professionalism and business judgment.

Body art, tattoos and piercing that have religious, ethnic or cultural meaning fall into a separate category.

If you have questions about the appropriateness of body art, tattoos and piercing as a "self-expression" or religious, ethnic or cultural statement, contact your company representative for clarification.

During business hours, consider covering non-religious "self-expression" statements of body art and tattoos with attire or makeup and remove body piercing that can be visible on your:

- Face

- Neckline

- Arms

- Wrists

- Hands

- Waistline

- Thighs

- Legs

- Ankles

Professional image is more important in the 21st century than ever before. Appearance and body language always speak first. Appearances influence the opinions and perceptions others have of you.

When you interview on a company designated "business casual" day, and have been told by your interviewer you can dress business casual – do not. Always dress business and make a powerful impression.

Dressing professionally for your interview shows respect for yourself, your career, and the organization to which you are seeking employment. To a great extent, you are what you wear. Look authoritative, confident, and successful. Take the worry out of your interview image. Let it be your secret to success.

Show you mean business!

Interview Etiquette: 17 Rules for Interviewing

Your organization commits a considerable amount of time and resources to interviewing and recruiting employees. They need to identify your *knowledge*, *skills*, and *abilities* in order to determine whether you are the best candidate for the job.

Your goal is to demonstrate how your knowledge and experiences can be of value to your organization. Provide examples of how your knowledge, skills, and abilities will help position you as a qualified candidate for the job. Use examples of past performance, experiences, project management, special assignments, internships, hobbies, volunteer work, and other activities to assist you in communicating your achievements.

At your interview, your appearance is the first impression you make; your manners and professionalism become important afterwards. Usually, the combination of *appearance*, *manners*, and *professionalism* help form the interviewer's hiring decision. Learning the rules of interviewing will assist you in becoming more successful in achieving career goals.

17 Rules for Interviewing

Rule 1 – Appearance

Wear a professional business suit. It is *recommended* that women wear a skirt suit.

Rule 2 – Be On Time

The interviewer interprets your arrival of fifteen to twenty minutes early, as your interest, commitment, dependability, and professionalism. Being late can show the opposite.

Rule 3 – First Impression

Be kind to the receptionist. Do not smoke, use your cell phone, chew gum, or listen to a portable radio while you are waiting for your interview. You are being observed.

Rule 4 –Outer Coat

Do not wear your outer coat into the interview. Take your coat off after you have spoken to the receptionist.

Rule 5 – Introductions

If the interviewer uses both first and last name during introductions, use the last name when addressing him or her. Introduce yourself by the name you *prefer* to be called.

Rule 6 – Handshake

Give a confident handshake and smile when you shake hands. If you have sweaty palms dry them with a tissue prior to your introduction.

Rule 7 –Sitting Down

Do not sit down until you have been invited to do so. *Ask* where they would like you to sit.

Rule 8 – Preparing for the Interview

- What skills does the position require?

- What skills do you have that relate to the job description?

- What anecdotes can you tell about your knowledge, skills, and abilities that demonstrate your qualifications?

- Before the interview, identify two or three top-selling points you want the interviewer to know about you, and determine how to present them during the interview.

- Bring three copies of your resume, even though you know they already have a copy. Multiple resume copies prepare you for unexpected group interviews.

- Bring a leather writing portfolio and a quality ink pen.

- Review your resume prior to the interview. Be prepared to answer questions and explain any gaps during your employment.

- Prepare and memorize five to seven questions you can ask about the position.

- Research the department of interest and know who the key people are. Identify who has the power to hire you.

Rule 9 – Vocal Tone

Match your vocal tone to the interviewer. Do not talk too loud or whisper when you speak.

Rule 10 –Body Language

Avoid signs of negative or power body language:

- Slouching

- Avoiding Eye Contact

- Forced Smiles

- Swinging of Foot or Legs

- Crossing your Legs over your Thigh

- Hand or Finger Movements

Rule 11 –Eye Contact

Make eye contact, show self-confidence, and answer questions directly with a clear enthusiastic voice. Look directly at the interviewer when answering questions or asking a question.

Take a moment to reflect before answering a difficult question. If you do not understand a question, ask for clarification. Listen; communication is two-way. If you are talking too much, you might miss important information about the position.

Rule 12 – Be Positive

Do not make any negative comments about your current position, management, co-workers, or former employers.

Rule 13 – Show You Want the Job

Show initiative, give examples of your ability to be a team player, work independently, solve problems, and perform the job.

Rule 14 – Close the Interview

Close the interview by asking the interviewer if they have any concerns about your ability to perform the job. Overcome any objections and "*ask for the job.*" Wait for a response, thank the interviewer and ask about the next step in the interview process.

Rule 15 – Be Natural

Be calm and natural during the interview closing.

Rule 16 –Thank You Letter

After the interview mail a *typed* thank you letter within twenty-four hours. Thank each interviewer in a separate letter for taking time to meet with you. Make sure you have the correct spelling of their names and titles. In your thank you letter, identify two to four points your interviewer liked in bullet format. Use *spelling* and *grammar* check, and *re-read* your letter before mailing. Do not use your organizations in-house letterhead or mailing system even if you are interviewing within your current organization.

Rule 17 – Follow Up

Contact your interviewer within one week unless otherwise instructed as to your interview status.

17 Powerful Interview Questions

Introduction

Interview preparation requires a successful strategy to obtain an offer for a new career opportunity. Preparation starts with the candidate researching the organization and identifying the company mission, goals, products, services, customers, and locations.

Whether you have a phone screening interview or one in person, preparation is the key to moving forward in the interview process. Candidates who prepare quality questions will be remembered. Often candidates ask few or no questions about the job. A lack of questions signals the interviewer you have given little or no thought about the position.

Interviewers who do all the talking have no opportunity to assess your skills and strengths. Take control of the interview by responding to questions with "examples" of your achievements. People in general remember short stories. "Paint a Picture" by communicating your ability to perform the job based on past achievements.

Example. At XYZ Company I consolidated our weekly and monthly reports and reduced overtime pay by…

Example. At XYZ Company my department increased customer service orders by…

Your goal in closing the interview is to answer the question in the hiring managers mind "Why Should I Hire You"? Asking quality questions engages the interviewer; providing examples of your skills sets you apart from the competition thereby positioning you as a candidate of choice.

17 Powerful Interview Questions

There are many questions you should ask during an interview. Your goal is to gather valuable information you need to determine if this position is a good career move for your future.

Although you may not think to ask every question about the position, asking questions that are important to your role is essential in making an employment decision. Often candidates are not called back for a second interview, because they have shown no interest in the position other than wanting or needing employment.

Salary usually does not come up in a first interview. If it does and you are asked about salary expectations, it is recommended you not state an amount, rather ask about the salary *range*. When you ask about the range you prevent yourself from possibly losing income as illustrated below.

Candidate 1:

Hiring Manager: What salary are you expecting for this position?

Candidate: I want a salary of $100,000 per year.

Hiring Manager: Great, that sounds good.

Candidate 2:

Hiring Manager: What salary are you expecting for this position?

Candidate: Could you tell me what the salary range is for this position?

Hiring Manager: The salary range is between $100,000–$110,000 per year.

Candidate: Based on my experience I believe $110,000 per year is appropriate.

Your income might not start at $110,000 per year, but starting at the high range increases your chances of negotiating a desired income based on your ability to perform the job. When you start with a lower salary it's difficult to increase what you initially stated you wanted. Candidate 1 possibly has lost $10,000 per year. The goal of the hiring manager is to get the most qualified candidate and if possible save their organization money.

Write and remember five to seven quality questions to ask at each interview. The responses to your questions will indicate if this position is the right match for your knowledge, skills and abilities.

Interview Questions

1. Skills

Where do you see my professional skills in this position?

2. Changes

What changes, if any, would you like to see implemented in this position?

3. Goals

What goals do you have for this position and how can my knowledge, skills, and abilities help you achieve them?

4. Management

To whom would I directly report in this position? Would I be reporting to more than one person? If so, whom?

5. Leadership

What type of leadership and personality are you looking for to fill this position?

6. Expectations

What expectations do you have for this position in my first 90 days?

7. Team workers

With whom will I be closely working on a daily basis?

8. Core competency skills

What specific core competency skills do I have that are of value to you and XYZ Corporation?

9.   **Challenges**

Are there any immediate challenges I will need to address in my first 90 days?

10.   **Projects**

Are there any pending projects that I should give priority to?

11.   **Business tools**

Will there be a laptop computer, cell phone, or pager available to me in this position?

12.   **Home office**

In this position, will I have the flexibility to work at my home office?

13.   **Employees**

How many employees would be reporting to me? Are all of these employees in good standing with the company?

14.   **Business reports**

What types of weekly, monthly, or quarterly reports will be required?

15.   **Overcome objections**

Do you have any questions or concerns about my ability to successfully perform this position that I can address for you today?

16.   **Close – "ask for the job"**

I'm excited about this position and the opportunity to use the skills you identified will be valuable to XYZ Corporation. *May I have the job?* Or, *May I have this career opportunity?*
Silence. Remain silent until the interviewer responds to your question. Silence is powerful.

17.   **Close — the next step**

What is the next step in the interview process? Will I have another opportunity to discuss my skills in more detail?

Closing

- Business card ~ Ask the interviewer for their business card.

- Thank you ~ Thank the interviewer for their time.

- Thank you letter ~ Send a typed thank you letter within 24 hours restating skills they identified will be valuable and your ability to perform the job.

- Email thank you's ~ Send an email thank you within 24 hours if a hiring decision will be made within the next 3 days.

- Follow-up ~ If you do not hear from your contact in the time they informed you, call or send an email of your continued interest in the position.

- No replies ~ If you do not hear from your interview contacts after three attempts, move on to another career opportunity.

- New opportunities ~ Always have multiple career opportunities in the pipeline. Do not limit yourself to one position.

Power Business Meals

Introduction

Every day a power meal is used for breakfast, lunch, teatime, and dinner. Professionals use power meals for interviews, promotions, meetings, conferences, meeting clients, presenting products and services, networking, and other reasons.

Today, corporations, associations, government agencies, United States military, politicians, attorneys, pharmaceutical, hospitality, and transportation industries, and entrepreneurs use formal and informal dining to conduct business.

Table manners play an important role in making a positive impression. Visible signs of your manners are essential to your professional success. Your social skills are on display; never assume others will not notice or be understanding of poor table manners. Polished table manners speak volumes about your professionalism, and can take your career or business to another level.

Business Dining Etiquette

Napkin use

- Place your unfolded napkin on your lap.
- The napkin remains on your lap during the entire meal.
- Use your napkin to gently blot your mouth during your meal.
- At the end of the meal, place your napkin to the right of your dinner plate.
- Do not refold or bundle up your napkin.

Ordering

- Ask your server questions you might have about the menu.
- As a guest, do not order one of the most expensive items on the menu.
- Women's orders are usually taken before men's.
- Your server will determine how to take your order.

The Pre-Set Table Setting

As a general rule, liquids are on your right side and solids are on your left.

To the right

- Glassware
- Cup and saucer
- Knives and spoons
- Seafood fork, if seafood is included in the meal

To the left

- Bread and butter plate
- Small butter knife is placed horizontally across the top of the plate
- Salad plate
- Napkin and forks

Use of silverware

- The rule of silverware usage is to work your silverware from the outside in.

- Use one utensil for each course.

- The salad fork is on the outer left, followed by your dinner fork.

- Your soup spoon is on your outer right, followed by your dinner knife.

- Dessert spoon and fork are placed above your plate or brought out with dessert.

American vs. European Style

American style

- Cut food by holding your knife in the right hand and the fork in the left hand.

- Change your fork from your left hand to your right hand to eat, with the fork tines facing down.

- If you are left-handed, keep your fork in your left hand, tines facing up.

European (or Continental) style

- Cut food by holding your knife in your right hand while securing your food with your fork in your left hand.

- Your fork remains in your left hand, tines facing down.

- Your knife is in your right hand.

- Eat small pieces of food.

- Pick food up with your fork, which is in your left hand.

When you have finished your meal

- Do not push your plate away from you.

- Lay your fork and knife diagonally across your plate.

- Place your knife and fork side by side with the sharp side of the blade facing inward. The fork tines should face down. The knife and fork should be positioned at 10 and 4 o'clock.

- Do not place used silverware back on the table. Place it on the saucer. Unused silverware should be left on the table.

- Leave a soup spoon on your soup plate.

Business Table Manners

- Doggy bag: Do not ask for a doggy bag if you are a guest. Reserve doggy bags for informal dining.

- Finger foods: Finger foods can be messy and are best left for informal dining. Order foods that can be eaten with a knife and fork.

- Alcoholic beverages: Use good judgment. Behavior patterns tend to change when you drink. If you are employed, drinking during business hours is not recommended.

- Smoking: Do not smoke while dining out; this might offend your guest. People form opinions of you based on what they see.

- Body language: Do not slouch; sit up straight at the table.

- Resting your hands: When you are not eating, keep your hands in your lap or resting on the table, with your wrists on the edge of the table. Elbows on the table are acceptable between courses but not during meals.

- Food seasoning: Do not season your food before you have tasted it.

- Chewing: Never chew with your mouth open or make noises when you eat. Do not talk with your mouth full.

- Slurping your soup: Do not slurp your soup from the spoon or pick the bowl up to your mouth. Spoon your soup away from you when you take it out of the bowl. Do not blow your soup if it is hot; wait for it to cool.

- Food between your teeth: If you cannot remove the food between your teeth with your tongue, excuse yourself from the table and go to the rest room where you can remove the food in private. Those foods might include broccoli, spinach, fresh ground pepper, or corn on the cob.

- Eating bread and rolls: Tear and butter one piece at a time.

- Conversation: Engage in lively conversation free of controversial topics such as politics, race, religion, or sex.

- Leaving the table: If you leave the table during the meal, simply excuse yourself.

- Out of your reach: If you need something on the table that is out of your reach, politely ask the person closest to the item to pass it to you.

- Fallen silverware: If a piece of silverware falls on the floor, pick it up if you can reach it. Politely ask the server to bring you a replacement.

- Food and liquid spills: If food spills off your plate, pick it up with a piece of your silverware and place it on the edge of your plate. If a liquid spills, clean it up as much as you can, and limit the attention you draw to yourself.

- Bad food: Never spit out a piece of bad food or gristle into your napkin. Discreetly remove the food from your mouth with your utensil and place it on the edge of your plate. You may choose to cover it up with other food on your plate.

- Dry mouth: Keep your mouth moist. A dry mouth can cause white saliva deposits to appear on your lips, and in the corners of your mouth without your knowledge.

Thank You Etiquette

There are many people with whom you interact daily. Saying "thank you" is important and effective in building relationships in interviews, business, with co-workers, internal and external customers, and clients. Thanking others makes a positive reflection on your business or organization's ability to succeed and achieve goals.

A thank you card can be displayed on a desk of a business associate as a reminder of your appreciation and admired by others. Thank you letters are recommended after an interview and expected when conducting business with others.

It's the little things that count, and pay off in a big way.

- Clients provide new and repeat business, referrals, and references for additional business.

- Co-workers usually provide assistance when working on projects and other daily tasks.

- Managers and supervisors provide support, feedback, and leadership for your career.

- Vendors or contractors: It is often teamwork that helps you achieve your departmental goals.

- Gifts: Be gracious when receiving gifts, even if you don't like what you receive.

Thank You Customs

Thank you gifts and customs vary based on culture.

Written Thank-you Notes

- Written thank you notes are more personal and convey special appreciation.

- Short two- or three-line messages are sufficient.

- Timely thank-you notes are sincere and easier to write when done within one week.

- Make a specific reference to the gift or contribution your business or organization received.

- Thank-you notes are for "thank-yous," not for business discussions.

Power Business Image: Show You Mean Business!

Planning your business wardrobe is essential in conveying you are serious about your profession and career. Every professional should have quality business suits and coordinates in his or her wardrobe. A tailored navy blue, black, or dark gray suit makes a powerful first impression. Add a business blouse for women and a shirt and tie for men to "show you mean business" in the eyes of management, your peers, customers, or clients.

Although women's pant suits are widely accepted in business, a "skirt suit" is advisable and more favorable to make a powerful first impression. However, pant suits (if appropriate for the work environment) add an alternative business or business casual look.

Whether you are working in a boardroom, courtroom, or in the office, or if you are meeting clients, attending meetings, or networking, your attention to detail is crucial to your success. Always be consistent in your appearance. A professional image is important when representing clients, presenting products and services and building long-term strategic relationships.

These professions might include:

- Administrative professionals
- Association professionals
- Attorneys and Legal professionals
- Bank and financial institution professionals
- Board members
- Chamber of commerce professionals
- Communications professionals
- Consultants
- County, State, and Federal Government employees
- CPAs and Accounting professionals
- Customer services professionals
- Education professionals

- Engineering and technology professionals
- Food service professionals
- Healthcare services professionals
- Hospitality professionals
- Human Resources professionals
- Marketing professionals
- Pharmaceutical professionals
- Public Relations professionals
- Sales and corporate executives: District, General, Regional Management, Executives and Vice Presidents
- Secretaries and Administrative professionals
- Social Services professionals

Men

Suit

- Solids, stripes, or plaids
- Matching jacket and trousers in the same fabric
- Trousers cuffed

Shirt

- Modified spread collar (recommended)
- Solids, stripes, or plaids
- Long-sleeved

Tie

- Solid, stripes, or small patterns
- Conservative (avoid political, religious, and sexual humor styles)
- Red is the color of power

Shoes

- Lace-ups only
- Dark color
- Polished and in good condition

Socks

- Dark solid colors or small patterns
- Match to trousers or shoes
- Mid-calf
- Cover white socks with dark socks

Belt

- Match to trousers or shoes
- No braces (suspenders) with a belt

Jewelry

- Earrings - not recommended
- Bracelets - not recommended

Hair

- Cut and styled
- Facial hair trimmed and groomed

Fragrance

- Conservative application
- Be considerate of those who may have allergies

Nail Care

- Manicured
- Neatly trimmed
- Clear polish (optional)

Attaché Case (Optional)

- Leather
- Dark color – preferably black
- Stylish
- Not oversized

Business Tools

- Leather writing tablet – dark color
- Quality ink pen (name engraving adds a personal touch)
- Your business card
- Professional name badge
- Cell phone or pager – TURN OFF during business meetings and conferences

Women

Suit

- Conservative
- Skirt or pant suit in the same fabric
- Fashionable basics

Blouse

- Solids, small prints or stripes
- Crew neckline, mock or regular turtlenecks

Shoes

- Classic leather pumps
- Closed-toe and closed-toe sling back styles
- Polished and in good condition

Jewelry

- No ankle bracelets

Hair

- Professionally styled
- No fashion hair colors

Hose

- Coordinated with attire
- No bare legs (no exception for summer)

Makeup

- Conservative application

Fragrance

- Conservative
- Be considerate of those who may have allergies.

Nail Care

- Manicured or acrylic – no chipped nail polish
- No fashion bright colors, studs or black nail polish
- No long nails

Attaché Case (Optional)

- Leather
- Dark color – preferably black
- Stylish
- Not oversized

Business Tools

- Leather writing tablet – dark color
- Quality ink pen (name engraving adds a personal touch)
- Your business card
- Professional name badge
- Cell phone or pager. TURN OFF during business meetings and conferences

Casual Looks for Men and Women

What Not to Wear

There are many definitions and opinions regarding what types of attire fall in the category of business casual. When in doubt, dress up a notch on the conservative side rather than the casual side, or ask your company representative. Listed are general guidelines for attire, accessories, and styles that are not considered business casual.

Athletic wear, athletic shoes, denim (jeans and jean shirts of any color), sweatshirts, sweatpants, exposed midriffs, leather wear, skorts / shorts / bermuda shorts, capri pants, uncovered sleeveless clothing, tee shirts, tanks, or tube tops, spaghetti straps and/or sun dresses, leggings and/or spandex pants, exposed cleavage, sheer clothing, short-sleeved shirts, bandanas, hats, ankle bracelets, fashion hair colors, baggy or oversized and undersized clothing, untucked shirts, military camouflage looks, swimwear, loungewear, nightwear looks, flannel pajamas, bare legs, moccasins, mid-calf strappy sandals, clogs, any color flip flops, visible body art, tattoos and piercings

Body art, tattoos and piercing are no longer reserved for bikers and sailors. These forms of non-religious "self-expression" statements have made their way to the boardroom and general population of organizations. However, self-expression statements can cross the business line and form unfavorable perceptions about your professionalism and business judgment.

Body art, tattoos and piercing that have religious, ethnic or cultural meaning fall into a separate category.

If you have questions about the appropriateness of body art, tattoos and piercing as a "self-expression" or religious, ethnic or cultural statement, contact your company representative for clarification.

During business hours, consider covering non-religious "self-expression" statements of body art and tattoos with attire or makeup and remove body piercing that can be visible on your:

- Face
- Neckline
- Arms
- Wrists
- Hands
- Waistline
- Thighs
- Legs
- Ankles

Business image is more important in the 21st century than ever before. Appearance and body language always speak first. Appearances influence the opinions and perceptions others have of you. Never underestimate the power your image has with those who you meet and conduct business with. In general, people tend to trust, have more confidence, and are loyal to professionals who look good.

Dressing professionally shows you have respect for yourself and for the organization you represent. To a great extent, you are what you wear. Look authoritative, confident, credible, and successful. Take the worry out of your business image. Let it be your secret to success.

Show You Mean Business!

Power Business Casual: Show You Mean Business!

Introduction

Business casual attire varies from one organization and industry to another. When distinguishing the differences between business casual and casual attire the keyword is "business". Without the prefix employees may tend to dress in attire that is more suitable for "casual wear" also known as "weekend wear".

Business casual may be defined as: *"Attire that provides a professional image which is appropriate for work and work-related events and conforms to company business casual dress policy guidelines."*

Casual attire is a separate image category and is often confused with business casual. Casual wear is usually reserved for those industries and business cultures such as Internet, tech savvy, and other similar companies. Casual attire is usually defined by each organization that provides a designated casual workday or casual business environment. These employees may have little or no interaction with the public. Casual dress guidelines are informal and have few attire restrictions. Organizations that have a casual attire workplace are usually specific about what is acceptable at work.

Summer Business Casual

Summer business casual attire provides the opportunity for employees to wear lightweight fabrics and seasonal colors and styles. The climate does not dictate that employees can dress less professional; however it does provide seasonal business choices. When coordinating your wardrobe for work, the same business casual policy guidelines apply throughout the year.

This chapter was written to provide a better understanding of the distinct differences between business casual and casual attire. Ultimately, employees should manage their careers and take ownership of their business casual image. Every professional has the responsibility to wear attire that is appropriate for work and promotes career success.

If you have questions about your organization's Business Casual dress policy guidelines, contact your company representative or Human Resources Department.

Today many organizations have a designated business casual day for their employees. These professions might include:

- Administrative professionals
- Association professionals
- Attorneys and Legal professionals
- Bank and financial institution professionals
- Board members
- Chamber of commerce professionals
- Communications professionals
- Consultants
- County, State, and Federal Government employees
- CPAs and Accounting professionals
- Customer services professionals
- Education professionals
- Engineering and technology professionals

- Food service professionals

- Healthcare services professionals

- Hospitality professionals

- Human Resources professionals

- Marketing professionals

- Pharmaceutical professionals

- Public Relations professionals

- Sales and corporate executives: District, General, Regional Management, Executives and Vice Presidents

- Secretaries and Administrative professionals

- Social Services professionals

How Do I Look?

Your image and everything you say and do should create the perception that you are professional, intelligent, reliable, skilled, trustworthy and polished. As you prepare your work wardrobe for each business casual day ask yourself:

1. Does my image make me feel and look respected?

2. With whom am I meeting today? Will I be meeting a customer, vendor or visitor at my location or theirs? If either applies, it is recommended you dress "business", although it may be your company business casual day. When meeting with a client at their location on their designated business casual or casual day dress in business attire. You never know what other guests may be attending your meeting without your knowledge.

3. Does my image prepare me for unannounced meetings, internal or external visitors?

4. Does my image help position me for promotions?

5. Does my image attract the wrong type of attention?

6. Does my image help identify me to take a possible leadership role in the absence of management?

7. Does my image promote career success or failure?

Business Casual for Men

Listed are business casual guidelines for planning your work wardrobe. Create your own style by adding your favorite colors and accessories that will enhance your image and personalize your look.

Suit or Coordinates

- Solids, stripes or plaids
- Suit or coordinates
- Trousers cuffed

Shirt

- Modified spread or buttoned collar
- Solids, stripes, or plaids
- Long-sleeved
- Short Sleeve shirts cover with a jacket

Tie (optional)

- Solid, stripes or small patterns
- Fashionable classics
- No political, religious, or sexual humor styles

Shoes

- Lace-ups or slip-ons
- Black or brown shoes
- Polished and in good condition

Socks

- Dark solid colors or small patterns
- Match to trousers or shoes
- Mid-calf
- Cover white socks with dark socks

Belt

- Match to trousers or shoes
- No braces (suspenders) with a belt

Jewelry

- Earrings - not recommended (casual)
- Bracelets - not recommended (casual)

Hair

- Clean cut styles
- Professionally cut and styled
- Facial hair trimmed and groomed

Fragrance

- Conservative application
- Be considerate of those who may have allergies

Nail care

- Manicured
- Neatly trimmed
- Clear polish (optional)

Quick image tips

- Tone on tone attire can create a nightclub look
- No white or beige business shoes
- No athletic shoes
- Sandals (not recommended)
- Always dress business for an interview

Attaché/carrying case (optional)

- Leather
- Black or dark brown
- Stylish
- Not oversized

Power Business Tools

- Leather writing tablet (black or dark brown with two business cards holders)
- Quality ink pen and pencil set (name engraving adds a personal touch)
- Your business card
- Professional name badge
- Cell phone or pager. *Turn off* during business meetings and conferences.

Business Casual for Women

Listed are business casual dress guidelines for planning your work wardrobe. Create your personal style by adding your favorite colors and accessories that will enhance your image and uniqueness.

Suit or coordinates

- Fashionable classics
- Skirt or pant suit in the same fabric
- Skirt or pant coordinates

Blouses/tops/sweaters

- Solids, small prints or stripes
- Crew neckline, mock or regular turtlenecks
- Sweater sets

Shoes

- Fashionable classic styles
- Pumps, sling back styles or flats
- Sandal styles (optional – use good judgment)
- Polished and in good condition

Jewelry

- No ankle bracelets
- Do not over accessorize

Hair

- Clean cut styles
- Professionally cut and styled
- No fashion hair colors (e.g., red, purple, blue, etc.)

Hose

- Coordinated with attire
- No bare legs (no exception for summer)
- No designer patterns such as fishnet styles

Make-up

- Conservative application

Fragrance

- Conservative
- Be considerate of those who may have allergies

Nail care

- Manicure or acrylic fill. No chipped nail polish.
- No fashion bright colors, studs or black nail polish
- No long nails

Quick image tips

- A low neckline can expose your breast line when you lean forward
- Very short attire attracts the wrong attention
- Red is the color of power
- Always dress business for an interview

Attaché case/carrying case (optional)

- Leather
- Black or dark brown
- Stylish
- Not oversized

Power business tools

- Leather writing tablet (black or dark brown with two business card holders)
- Quality ink pen and pencil set (name engraving adds a personal touch)
- Your business card
- Professional name badge
- Cell phone or pager. *Turn off* during business meetings and conferences.

Casual Attire for Men and Women: What Not to Wear for Business Casual

Employees who choose to wear casual attire regardless of the dress policy do so at the risk of limiting their career opportunities. Taking the initiative to improve your image will increase your chances of being promoted and make you more marketable inside and outside of your organization.

There are outlet and discount stores, seasonal sales, weekend and holiday sales, and resale shops available to purchase fashionable affordable attire on a budget. Before you wear any of the listed attire, consider your career, the amount of money you want to make and ask yourself will this attire advance my career. Listed are styles, accessories and looks that are considered casual.

Casual Attire and Accessories

Athletic wear, athletic shoes, denim (jeans and jean shirts of any color), sweatshirts, sweatpants, exposed midriffs, leather wear, skorts / shorts / bermuda shorts, capri pants, uncovered sleeveless clothing, tee shirts, tanks, or tube tops, spaghetti straps and/or sun dresses, leggings and/or spandex pants, exposed cleavage, sheer clothing, short-sleeved shirts, bandanas, hats, ankle bracelets, fashion hair colors, baggy or oversized and undersized clothing, untucked shirts, military camouflage looks, swimwear, loungewear, nightwear looks, flannel pajamas, bare legs, moccasins, mid-calf strappy sandals, clogs, any color flip flops, visible body art, tattoos and piercings

Meetings and Conferences

Business Casual Attire

In every business situation your supervisor, management, and your peers are observing you. Never underestimate the importance of a meeting simply because it has been designated a business casual event. What you wear or the lack of what you wear will affect your career success. Use this event to showcase how well you manage your image.

Professional Conduct

During most events time is usually designated for networking or entertainment. When alcoholic beverages are available, although it is a personal and business decision, consider having non-alcoholic beverages. Each person's tolerance for alcohol varies; personalities, language, and behavior patterns can change. From an employer's perspective, if you cannot manage your behavior how can they trust you to manage others in your organization? Any inappropriate actions can be a career-limiting move for your future. Use good judgment, be a good listener and observer, be sociable, and have fun.

Summary

What you wear to work has everything to do with how successful you will be throughout your career. The next generation of professionals and business culture is rapidly changing. With change comes attire that may tend to be more casual and less professional; however the basic business rules for image have not changed. These rules include knowing what attire to wear, when to wear it, and why you should wear it.

One of the most important non-verbal communications is how your image silently speaks for you. Wear attire that gets you noticed for the right reasons, compliments you, and will help you accomplish your short- and long-term career goals.

Be consistent in your professional attire by branding your career image. Create a Power Business Casual image that will take you to the next career level, and have others asking about your secret to success.

Show You Mean Business!

Power of Employment: 27 Secrets to Survive Your First 90 Days of Employment

Introduction

The powerful 27 Secrets have helped many professionals survive their first 90 days of employment and have provided a foundation for career growth. These are secrets you are expected to know. No one intentionally plans to fail—people fail because they lack knowledge and information. Knowledge provides the ability for you to apply the information you have learned. The 27 Secrets will enable you to join the ranks of those who have successfully used these secret tools and strategies throughout their careers.

Starting a new job is one of the most stressful experiences people face. The first 90 days of employment are crucial to your career success—whether you are a current professional seeking new employment, a college or high school graduate seeking employment for the first time, or a previously unemployed person re-entering the workforce.

Information you provide to an employer about your knowledge, abilities, integrity, and communication skills will be put to the test. Before you speak, think about what you are going to say. Choose your words carefully, and be aware of your body language so that you are not misunderstood. Observe your environment while you are adjusting to your new role, responsibilities, people, and organizational culture.

Manage your internal social network by getting to know multiple people in an organization before you align yourself with any one person or group of people. People judge you by the company you keep. When you are new to an organization, you have no knowledge of other professionals' reputations. In business, what you don't know *can* hurt you. Take your time, be perceptive, and use good judgment.

During new hire orientation and training, be positive and upbeat; be a good listener and communicator. Get involved by participating—be a team player, and take a leadership role in training activities. Manage your attitude, behavior, and interactions with management and co-workers. Management will evaluate you based on your ability to perform your job and on your written, verbal, and non-verbal communication skills. At the end of your probationary period, they will determine if you are the right fit for the job and organization based on what they see and feedback from others.

Maintain a level of professionalism, and marketability in your new and future positions. Be dependable, approachable, and enthusiastic about your new career. Demonstrate your ability to manage and complete assignments and solve problems. Make a commitment to contribute to the success of organizational goals.

Secret 1: Business Image

The professional image you presented to get hired should be consistent throughout your career. Always dress for your *next* job.

- Dress professionally every day.

- Attire that is too short, tight, or revealing should not be worn to work.

- Do not dress as if you are going to an entertainment club, evening on the town, or away for the weekend.

- Uniforms should be clean and pressed. Even wash and wear clothing usually requires a light pressing.

- Self expression art, such as piercings and tattoos, are inappropriate for business and should not be visible. Remove them or cover them up with make-up or clothing.

- If you are unsure if you should wear it or expose it, do not.

Secret 2: First Day at Work

- Arriving fifteen minutes early will make a good impression.

- Be friendly, positive, and focused.

- Prepare yourself for a long day; be prepared to complete new hire paperwork.

- Bring a pen with black ink and a writing tablet.

Secret 3: New Hire Orientation

- Introduce yourself to management and others.

- Be open to changes and new challenges.

- Be aware of your vocal tone when you speak; match your vocal tone to the speaker.

- Bring personal information you need for identification, automatic deposit, insurance, and other benefits.

Secret 4: Employment At-Will Policy

- Employment At-Will policy states either an employee or the company can terminate an employee's employment, with or without cause, or with or without advance notice.

- Employment At-Will is usually stated on your job application, and in your letter of offer for employment. If you work for an Employment At-Will employer and require clarification, ask your manager or a human resources representative.

Secret 5: Employment Expectations

- Ask for a copy of your job description if you do not have one.

- Ask questions about your role, responsibilities, and expectations of your performance.

- If you are sick, will be late for work, or have a personal emergency, contact your immediate supervisor and advise them of your situation. Leave a voice mail message and an e-mail message specifying the time you plan to arrive for work.

Secret 6: Workplace Profanity

There are no excuses or exceptions for using profanity or words that translates to curse words. The use of the word "freakin" or other slang words shows your lack of maturity, character, intelligence, emotional control, and professionalism.

Secret 7: Employee Internet Search

- If a new or potential employer did an Internet search on you, what would they find out about you? Do not allow your past or future behavior to sabotage your career.

- Think twice before you participate in social activities that might appear on Internet sites.

- Information on the Internet is difficult to remove. Be prepared to explain comments and pictures that are unfavorable about your character.

- You could risk losing your job or a career opportunity if your employer has concerns about your perception to management, co-workers and clients.

Secret 8: Company Surveillance

More than eighty percent of companies monitor their employees' communications and whereabouts. You have no privacy at work. Be selective with your choice of words in written communication to others. Do not think your personal e-mails to co-workers, family, and friends are none of your employer's business during business hours.

The use of the company computer for your small business can get you terminated. It does not matter if you are on a break, at lunch, arrive early or stay late on your own time. Keep in mind the computer is the property of your employer.

Employers might observe you using any of the following resources:

- Blog surfing
- Web traffic
- Computer files
- Instant Messaging
- Interior and exterior cameras, visible or invisible to you
- Phone calls
- E-mails
- Satellite tracking of a company car or cell phone

Secret 9: Cell Phone Etiquette

At work, be mindful of your manager, co-workers, and your ability to get work done without cell phone interruptions on company time. There are several rules you should consider if you have a cell phone at work.

- Turn off your cell phone ringer. Set your cell phone on vibrate.

- Let your messages go to voice mail. Check your voice mail and text messages during your break or at lunch time. Avoid checking messages during company-sponsored meals.

- It is unprofessional to check voice mail or text messages in the presence of clients.

- Use your phone only for important and emergency calls. Social calls from family and friends are not considered important.

- Do not bring your cell phone to meetings. Acknowledging cell phone messages during meetings is disruptive, rude and unprofessional. Attention given to your messages is an indication to management that you are not focused on your job.

- Identify a private place to make cell phone calls. Do not stay at your desk and talk. Protect your privacy so your conversations are not overheard.

- Never use your cell phone in the restroom. You never know who is in the restroom. People on the other end can hear bathroom sounds such as toilets flushing and water running. Respect the privacy of others who may be using the restroom.

Secret 10: E-mail Etiquette

Electronic mail is the easiest method of communication. Your e-mail messages may be printed and distributed or forwarded to others. Make it easy for others to read your e-mail messages by remembering these tips:

- Be specific in your subject line to communicate what is in your message.

- Be clear and concise. State your purpose in your first paragraph. Include details that will help the reader respond to your message in a timely manner.

- Use proper grammar, punctuation and spell-check. Grammar and spell-checkers do not always catch all errors. Print and re-read your document before you send it.

- Be professional. Do not use suggestive e-mail or emoticons, symbols such as the smiley face, numbers or letters to indicate you are upset.

- Be mindful of your written communication tone. Come across as approachable, friendly and respectful. Never send "flame" e-mail to anyone when you are angry.

- Watch your manners at work. Communicate good manners by using please, thank you, excuse me, and I'm sorry when appropriate.

- Do not gossip, write negatively about other co-workers, or discuss inappropriate or non-business related subjects in e-mail. You never know who your e-mail messages may be forwarded to.

- Include your contact information. Add your full name, title, e-mail, and telephone and fax number.

Secret 11: New Hire Training

- Always be on time.
- Conduct yourself as a professional.
- Do not fall asleep in training.
- Participate and volunteer for training activities.
- Do not be loud or have late parties in your room or hotel lounge if you are off-site.
- Be confidential—keep your night out on the town and consumption of beverages to yourself.
- It is not advisable to have personal romances with co-workers or management.

Secret 12: Power Listening Skills

Listening is one of the most important communication skills. Effective communication is more about listening and less about talking.

- Listen to understand.
- Listen to avoid miscommunication.
- Observe body language – listen for what is not said.
- Listen with your eyes, ears, heart, and mind.
- Listen to understand assignments and what is expected of you.

How to Listen

- Maintain good eye contact.
- Do not interrupt the speaker.
- Confirm instructions and ask appropriate questions.

Secret 13: Cubicles—Open and Shared Workspace

What you display in your workspace communicates to others who you are and what you think.

- Be selective about what you display.
- Stay away from displaying items that might include social issues, sex, politics, and religion.
- Do not make your workspace look like your home.
- If you are single, be conscious of displaying a picture of your mate, as they may change.

Secret 14: Interpersonal Communication Skills

The purpose of communication is to share information. Clear communication is an essential element for success in the twenty-first century.

The keys to effective communication are to learn how to listen, speak clearly, and assert yourself with confidence. The ability to skillfully communicate confidently with people will set you apart from others.

Consider the following keys to effective communication:

- You must have the desire to communicate. Learn and understand the structure of the communication process.
- Master basic communication skills: connect with the person or audience, convey messages people understand, and check their responses for understanding.
- Practice to achieve effective communication skills. The more you practice, the easier it is to connect with people.
- Be patient. It takes patience and confidence to become a polished communicator.

The confident communicator:

- Develops an effective personal style.
- Exercises good eye contact and facial expressions.
- Uses appropriate hand gestures to convey a feeling of openness and ease.

Secret 15: Multicultural Communication

In the twenty-first century, women and minorities will constitute the great majority of the workforce. The global market demands knowledge, sensitivity, and understanding of the ways of other cultures.

- Feel comfortable with diversity.
- Recognize our similarities.
- See people as individuals instead of members of special groups.
- Learn about our differences by asking questions rather than observing them.

Secret 16: Office Politics

- Avoid participating in office politics.
- Stay neutral in your position and comments.
- If someone asks your opinion, simply state you have not made a decision or you have no comment.

Political and Social Issues

- Do not engage in conversations where you are expected to voice your opinion.
- It is advisable to keep your personal viewpoints private.
- Be a good listener.

Secret 17: Network at Work

Networking in the twenty-first century is more important for your career than ever before.

No matter where you work – a Corporation, a Government Agency, a Non-Profit Organization, or an Association – networking is important to your career.

Traditional career paths are rapidly changing. People must rely on their own ability to build networks at work and manage their own careers. "Social Networking" is a preferred alternative to traditional organizational charts and everyday business transactions.

Having a network of contacts–both inside and outside of an organization –is the most important thing a professional can do for their career. If you desire to get a promotion, spend time networking. It's Not Who You Know…It's Who Knows You!

Why Network at Work?

- Change – Use your network to stay informed about organizational change.

- Bottom Line – Your job depends on the success of the organization.

- Venture – Step into non-traditional career opportunities.

- Collaboration – Increase teamwork with other people and departments.

- Knowledge Expansion – Create a network of people with different interests and expertise.

Benefits

- Increased visibility. New opportunities will find you.

- Accountability and responsibility. Manage your "own" career.

- Options. Always keep your career options open.

Transitional Skills

- Determine a strategy to showcase your skills, abilities, and interest to others.

Secret 18: Know Your Organization and How It Works

Often employees work for the same organization for years without knowing important information such as the company website address. If your company has a website, it probably contains valuable information that can help you both professionally and personally.

Make it a regular practice to visit your company's website. Check the career section to learn about career opportunities, educational programs, and other areas of interest. Ask supervisors and managers questions about products and services you are not familiar with that may be beneficial to your success. You will discover the more you know, the more you can grow within your organization.

Know the Facts

- Website address
- Organization purpose
- Mission and vision statements
- History, growth and economic challenges
- Services, know what you do and why
- Organizational structure, departments and management
- How many locations and employees
- Culture
- Management philosophy, written and practiced

Secret 19: Time Management Strategies

Assessing Your Relationship with Time

Establishing your relationship with time is an important part of learning to use time wisely. Everyone's relationship with time is different; therefore, all strategies for managing time will vary accordingly.

Your strengths, weaknesses, commitments, lifestyle, and responsibilities all play a role in your time management strategy.

Priorities

- Identify your work priorities.

- Write down your priorities; be as specific as possible.

- Rank the importance of multiple priorities.

- Too many priorities at the same time will increase your stress.

Goals

- Translate your priorities into goals.

- Break each goal into activities and identify the steps needed to achieve the goal.

- Identify resources needed to accomplish your goal; you might require the assistance of other people.

Planning

- Use a monthly calendar. Your monthly calendar or notebook is a time-saving device. Consistent use of your calendar provides a visual reminder of your commitments.

- Identify work-related goals, such as weekly, monthly, or quarterly reports, and add them to your calendar.

- Schedule important activities such as teleconferences, meetings, appointments, due dates, and deadlines and add them to your calendar. Scheduling deadlines gives you direction and confirms your commitment to your deadlines.

- Plan time in your calendar to review and accomplish deadlines, but don't wait until the day before a deadline occurs.

- Highlight important dates on your calendar with a colorful marker.

Personal Time Management Barriers

- Do you feel "too controlled"?

- Is the task you need to accomplish boring?

- Identify your own barriers to effective time management.

Achieve "Meaningful" Outcomes

Effective time management will assist you in achieving meaningful outcomes, not more outcomes.

Secret 20: Sharing Too Much Information

- Be on your best behavior when you are in the same business and social settings as management.

- Your manager or supervisor might be in the same age group as you or younger. Do not drop your professional guard.

- When you relax in conversations with management you run the risk of sharing too much personal information about yourself.

- Protect your privacy so that others may not gain confidential information about your lifestyle.

Secret 21: Teamwork Strategies

Teamwork is bringing people together for the common purpose of maintaining and improving team member interactions within an organization.

- Listen. Listen to ideas and gain new ones.

- Questions. Ask questions to determine what to do and extend thinking.

- Persuade. Exchange, present, and sell your ideas.

- Help. Offer help and encouragement to team members.

- Respect. Respect the opinions of others on your team.

- Share. Share your ideas and thinking.

- Participate. Contribute actively to the team.

Secret 22: Why You Should Have a Mentor

There are many organizations that have mentor-protégé programs for matching new hires to established employees. According to career experts, anyone who is to have a successful career should have a mentor. Some professional organizations may have mentor programs. Take the initial steps by establishing contact with potential mentors.

Mentors can provide some advantages. They can:

- Help you adjust to new people, environment, policies, and procedures.
- Provide guidance and helpful career advice.
- Introduce you to industry key contacts.
- Invite you to leadership and industry events.
- Help you elevate your career at a faster pace.

Secret 23: Career Coach: Get Advice from a Professional

A career coach can help alleviate the overwhelming stress associated with employment or promotions. Whether you are starting a new career, job searching, recovering from a job loss, or re-entering the workforce, obtaining the advice of a career coach can provide invaluable knowledge and expertise. Although a career coach is a personal choice, consider these benefits that other professionals have benefited from.

- Confidential career advice
- Tools and strategies to manage internal customers and organizational politics.
- Career crisis prevention and intervention advice
- Problem-solving strategies
- Advancement strategies for climbing the corporate ladder
- Identification of hidden skills you can use at work
- Assistance with negotiating employment offers and promotions.

Secret 24: Build Good Relationships with Management

Building relationships with management should be a part of your career development strategy. Managers look for employees who show a sincere interest in setting and achieving goals, self growth, and improvement. Employees who accept additional assignments, volunteer for special projects, and help others are positioning themselves for advancement and management support for new career opportunities.

Management Relationship Strategies

- Build good relationships with management
- Invite your manager or supervisor to break or lunch
- Resolve conflicts
- Ask for additional responsibilities
- Volunteer for assignments
- Be seen as an asset
- Develop your management network

Secret 25: Understand What Is Expected of You

Take time to understand what is expected of you in existing and future career roles. Review your job description with your supervisor, and identify new skills you can learn and others you can improve upon to successfully complete your probationary period. The knowledge and skills you learn will position you for your *next* job.

It is essential you take the initiative to meet with your supervisor in 30, 60, and 90 days to gain valuable feedback about your performance. Ask what skills can be improved and what steps are necessary to accomplish the skills they have identified. Let your supervisor be your "champion" for your career development, but never forget that it is ultimately up to you to manage your own career. Listen and be open to critique that will enable you to improve and acquire new skills, use the resources available to achieve department goals, and increase your visibility.

Knowledge, Skills, And Abilities (KSAs) / Core Competencies

- What skills will I need for professional development?
- What abilities do I have that require proficiency?
- What additional core competencies will I need to be successful?
- Always make your manager look good.
- Have one-on-one meetings with your manager on a regular basis.
- Contribute to your department goals.
- Identify department priorities and concerns.
- Identify who you can recruit in your "circle of influence" through "networking" to help you achieve your goals.

Technology Skills

- Know what skills are required.
- Be proficient in those skills.
- Learn new skills for promotional opportunities.

Secret 26: Intercultural Diversity Skills

The ability to maximize the knowledge, skills and abilities of multicultural workgroups will contribute to organizational goals.

- Knowledge. Have basic intercultural knowledge of patterns of communication, beliefs, values, and world views.
- Communication. Communicate effectively with individuals and diverse groups.
- Sensitivity. Be sensitive to others' perceptions in a multicultural environment.
- Conflict Resolution. Use cultural-specific knowledge to resolve conflict.

Secret 27: Career Exit Strategy

If you determine—before or at the end of your 90-day probationary period—that you are not a good match for the position and no longer want to work for the organization, here are some steps to assist you. These steps also apply if you have accepted a career opportunity with another organization.

Volunteer Resignation – Do

- Type a dated letter of resignation and present it to your manager.
- Give two weeks notice, and state your last day in the letter.
- Be prepared for your employer to ask you to leave immediately if this is during your probationary period or if you have accepted a job offer with a competitor.
- Ask what you can do to make your transition a smooth one.
- Wish your manager good luck in his or her career.
- Thank your manager for the career opportunity.

Do Not

- Send your resignation in an e-mail message.

- Walk out without giving notice.

- Brag about where you are going.

- Tell other people why you are leaving.

- Show up late, not show up at all, or call in sick after you have given notice unless you absolutely have to.

- Bad mouth your employer to your next career opportunity.

Termination

If you are terminated during or at the end of your probationary period or at some point in your career, the following guidelines may assist you.

- Ask why you are being terminated if you do not know.

- Accept the termination.

- Do not argue.

- Do not cry.

- Do not beg for your job back.

- Do not have a bad attitude, use profanity, throw things, or threaten anyone.

- Ask for a "Letter of Reference" on company letterhead if you have been downsized.

Whether you leave on your own terms, are terminated, or your position is eliminated, demonstrate the same professional behavior and attitude you used to get hired. Leave with class on a positive note. You never know when people you have worked with in the past may be in a position to hire, promote or make your life difficult at future career opportunities.

Summary

The most important thing you can do is take "ownership" of your career. Your employer is not responsible for providing all the training, tools, strategies and knowledge you need to be successful. How you present yourself during the first 30-, 60-, and 90-day probationary period will determine if you add value to the organization. Everything you say and do, how you interact, and how you are perceived by others play a role in your success.

If you do not have a college degree, consider obtaining one. Ask if your organization has a college assistance or tuition reimbursement program. If there is no college program, do not let that stop you from obtaining your education. A college degree will positively impact your financial future, worth, and give you the edge when applying and competing for other positions. It's not where you start but where you finish that counts.

Make a commitment to continued learning. Attend industry association meetings, seminars, training programs, and read books and periodicals. Become knowledgeable about your industry and related fields so you are well rounded.

The time, personal, and financial investment you make in your career is entirely up to you. The only limits you have are those you place on yourself. Establish yourself as a trustworthy, ethical, and credible expert in your field, and your reputation will follow you.

The Power of Office Etiquette

Introduction

Office etiquette offers practical advice and tips that are easy to use and helps you come across as a polished professional in a variety of business situations. There are many etiquette questions that might keep you wondering what to do or if you've done the right thing. Being unsure of what to do is uncomfortable. Knowledge builds certainty. Learning how to handle etiquette situations in the office, in open and shared spaces, through electronic communication; at an office party, and traveling on company business builds confidence.

People gravitate to those who are courteous, considerate, interesting, kind, professional, respectful, and thoughtful. The etiquette skills you develop will be valuable to you throughout your career and business life.

The Power of Office Etiquette

Office etiquette is a manner of professionalism and personal behavior by employees, to establish positive interaction between management, co-workers, clients and visitors. Knowledge and practice of office etiquette can help employees make a positive contribution to the organization by applying the following list of principles:

- Answering the phone. Always be polite and courteous when answering the phone. Your voice should be pleasant, sincere and express a concern for helping the caller.

- Chewing gum. Avoid chewing, blowing, and popping gum during business hours. This behavior is distracting and unprofessional when communicating with others. Using breath mints or similar products is a good alternative to chewing gum.

- Coughing, yawning, sneezing and belching. Although these are necessary body functions, they can be unhealthy and unattractive. Always cover your mouth or turn away if possible, to protect others from germs. Do not say "God bless you" when someone sneezes; his or her culture may not believe in God.

- Makeup. Use your break time or visits to the restroom to attend to your personal appearance.

- Body language. Use positive body language when communicating with others.

- Be tactful with rude people. When others are rude to you, be calm, patient, and courteous. Maintain your composure, and then respond professionally, politely, and positively.

- Personal conversations. Avoid personal conversations with friends, when co-workers or clients are waiting. Personal conversations should be brief and terminated when others approach you.

- Cell phones and pagers. Turn your cell phone and pagers off when you are working, attending meetings, conferences, and training and in work related conversations with others. Check your messages at break time and during lunch.

- Personal office visits. Discourage personal office visits by family and friends, except if there is an emergency.

- Be punctual. All workers should be punctual at the beginning of their workday, returning from breaks, lunch, and attending meetings, conferences, training, and other events.

- Annoying habits. There are distracting habits that others may find unpleasant, such as whistling, picking your nose, tapping your pencil or pen, talking to your computer and others. Identify your annoying habits and avoid doing them at work.

- Respect others. Treat everyone with respect. Never yell at or disrespect management or co-workers.

- Microwave foods. Be careful not to burn foods. Food odors such as popcorn usually carry a scent throughout the office.

- Smoking. If you smoke, identify and use designated smoking areas at work, meetings, conferences, training and other work-related events.

Cubicle and Open Space Etiquette

Today's office environment consists of cubicles and open workspaces. Personal office adjustments can mean the difference between a pleasant or frustrating atmosphere. Listed, are a few tips to help you be more comfortable with co-workers.

- First Impressions. Your cubicle and open workspace communicates to management, co-workers, and others about the type of worker you are. Make sure your space makes a good impression. Keep your area clean, tidy, and maintain well-organized documents. Watch what you post or display, people form opinions of you based on what they see.

- Greetings. Greet guests as they enter your workspace.

- Self-Awareness. Use good common sense; do not be too loud, intrusive or unpleasant.

- Cologne and perfume. Many people are allergic to colognes, perfumes and scented deodorants. If you choose to apply fragrance, keep your application light and softly scented.

- Food odors. You may think your food smells good, while others may not. If you eat onions or other foods with strong odors, use mints or brush your teeth and tongue after eating. Be considerate of others and know the rules for eating food or snacking at your desk.

- Confidential matters. In an open environment people do hear and listen to your conversations. Do not talk about confidential matters that you do not want other people to hear. Should you hear confidential matters, pretend that you haven't heard anything, and do not repeat what you have heard.

- Computer screen. Do not look at a person's computer screen without the co-worker's permission and knowledge. Do not use screen savers that make noise.

- Speak quietly. Do not talk loudly over partitions or to co-workers. Go to the person's cubicle or open workspace.

- Speaker phones. Do not use speaker phones at your desk. Other people may be distracted by your voice and your party's voice.

- Personal calls. Keep personal calls to a minimum.

- Phone interruptions. Do not interrupt a person who is on the phone, or use hand signals to distract them. Wait your turn, or come back when the call is finished.

- Interruptions. Do not walk into your co-worker's cubicle or designated open space without permission. When a co-worker is busy, pretend the door is closed. Contact your co-worker by phone or email, or ask if you could meet with them.

- Music. Ask about your organization's policy with regards to music in shared or open spaces. Be considerate of others who might not enjoy your music selection, or who find music distracting at work.

- Prevent distractions. If possible, arrange your desk away from your cubicle opening. Less eye contact can help eliminate distractions. When you make eye contact with someone at your cubicle, you have opened the door to communication. Be polite, but inform the person if this is not a good time, and arrange for a mutual time to meet.

- Conference room for meetings. If possible, reserve a conference or meeting room when you make appointments with clients or vendors. You want your guest to be comfortable and relaxed; therefore, you must provide excellent service. You should have privacy in order to conduct business without others listening.

- Respect meditation. Do not interrupt someone who appears to be meditating or in deep thought.

- Be cautious with foliage. Remember, others may have allergies to certain plants.

- Respect privacy. When sharing a space, suggest taking lunch and breaks at different times, if possible, to allow each of you some private and quiet time.

Electronic Mail Etiquette

Electronic mail is about communicating with other people. Composing an e-mail message requires that you read it over before sending it. Ask yourself what sort of response you want from the receiver. Time spent on making your communication clear is time well spent.

Regardless of the communication used, there are business guidelines and professional courtesies that should be followed. Because electronic communication is not in-person, it lacks voice inflection, tone, body language, and facial expression. Your choice of words is critical to e-mail communication.

Electronic communication has a significant impact on your business skills. You will need:

- A strong vocabulary

- Proper spelling and grammar.– re-read your message. Spelling and grammar checks may not always correct words that are spelled or used incorrectly.

- The ability to construct sentences to convey your message.

- Skills to express yourself clearly and concisely, both verbally and in writing.

Subject Lines

- Always include a subject line in your message.

- Avoid creative subject lines. A meaningful subject line provides the recipient with information about your message.

- Stay focused on the subject. The subject is the easiest way to follow the communication.

- Uppercase. Do not type your entire email in uppercase. In electronic mail this is considered "shouting" and can be difficult to read.

Replies

- When to reply. Reply to all email messages within twenty-four hours.

- Out of Office reply. Always use your "Out of Office reply" to inform others when you will be out of the office, when you will return, when to expect a reply, and a contact name and phone number of whom they can contact in your absence.

- Replying and changing the subject. When replying to a message put "Reply to" and your subject. If you are replying to a message and changing the subject, start a new message. Changing the conversation without changing the message can be confusing for the receiver.

- CC or Not to CC. There is no such thing as private email. Even when messages are deleted, many software programs can access messages from the hard drive. Before you click on "send", consider the content of your message, and about who may eventually read your message without your knowledge. Do not send personal or confidential emails. You would not want your message read or misunderstood by the wrong person.

- Addressing mail. Be careful to understand who will be receiving your reply. It could be embarrassing if your personal message ends up on a mailing list for everyone to read.

- No "flame" e-mail. Avoid messages sent in anger. E-mail is not the place to make negative comments. Negative comments can hurt people and your career.

- No replies. If your message does not require a response, let the recipient know. This can save time for both parties. Say something like "No Reply Necessary" at the end of your message.

- Thanks or OK. Do not send e-mails that say "Thanks" or "OK". One word replies can be interpreted as spam mail. When possible say "thank-you" in person or write a note.

- Website address. When sending a website address, always type it in the form of http:// because some programs will permit the user to click on the Web address to go directly to the site. Without the http:// prefix, some programs will not recognize it as an Internet address.

- Internet lingo. While you may be an Internet pro and familiar with Internet lingo and "emoticons" (like the popular smiley face ☺ and others), don't assume the recipient will understand.

- Attachments. Always use the subject line to inform the recipient of an attached document. Keep attachments to a minimum. The larger the attached document, the longer it takes to download. Consider faxing or mailing long documents, with the recipient's permission. When faxing or mailing documents, take ownership and confirm its receipt with the receiver.

- Forwarded messages. Put your comments at the top of the message. Refrain from sending messages that have been forwarded numerous times, start a new message.

- Signature. A signature usually contains your contact information. Many people use an automatic signature.

- Make sure your signature identifies who you are by listing your full name, phone, and fax number.

- Keep your signature short. Four to seven lines is the guideline for maximum lines in a signature.

Personal Hygiene Etiquette

Body odor

You should consult your doctor before using any products or have any concerns about your hygiene or health.

Body odor control tips

- Shower or bathe at least once per day.

- Use antiperspirant deodorant and body powder.

- Astringents used under the arms kill bacteria.

- Shaving or trimming underarm hair helps eliminates a breeding ground for bacteria.

- Launder clothing more often. Wash clothes using an odor-fighting detergent. Dry clean clothes on a regular basis.

- If the odor is stained in your clothing it will be difficult to remove the smell, even if you wash or use dry cleaning.

- Spicy foods, caffeine, and stressful situations will intensify body odor.

- Freshen-up. During the day freshen-up those areas of your body, which require more attention.

Halitosis (bad breath)

Consult your dentist if you have questions about the appropriate care for yourself. Bad breath can be caused by:

- Diet
- Gum disease
- Improper hygiene
- Smoking
- Some medications

Control bad breath by:

- Scheduling regular dental check-ups for consultation
- Using breath mints
- Using mouthwash
- Drinking plenty of water
- Using a tongue scraper

Office Party Etiquette

During the year you may be invited to your company office party. No matter how festive the occasion, it is important to remember this is business. Office parties and functions are the most likely career killers. Sometimes current and potential employees behave inappropriately. Do not risk your career success by damaging your professional reputation at any occasion.

The following advice will ensure a smooth and enjoyable celebration:

- Attend the office party. Attending the office party is the *politically correct* thing to do, and shows you are a team player. No matter how formal or informal the occasion, there is someone always watching your behavior and noting whether or not you attend.

- Who should attend? Clarify who is invited with the party coordinator. Spouses, children, boyfriends, and girlfriends are not always invited.

- Arrival and departure. Arrive on time and avoid arriving twenty minutes before the party ends just to make an appearance. Do not be the last to leave. Say goodbye to company officials. Your error in judgment will be noticed.

- Eat and drink. Eat something light before the party. If alcohol is served, drink in moderation and responsibly. It may be best not to drink at all.

- Dress appropriately. Dress professionally for the occasion. Anything *short, tight*, and *revealing* should stay at home.

- Introduce yourself. Your company party may be the only time you see the CEO, VPs, and other company officials in person. This may be a good opportunity to become visible.

- Conversations. Keep conversations light and happy. Do not use this occasion to criticize others or discuss work-related problems.

- Business romances. Work and work-related activities should involve no public display of affection. If you meet someone of interest, discreetly exchange your name and phone numbers and connect at a later date.

- Dancing. Remember, you are at work; be conscious of inappropriate body movements.

- Network. Use the occasion to strengthen new and old business acquaintances.

Travel Etiquette

Many employees will attend training, conferences, meetings, or special events at other locations. Unless you are management, you might be assigned a roommate. Listed are tips to help you have a positive roommate experience.

Tips for Roommates

- Communicate. Both talking and listening will be the key to a good roommate relationship.

- Identify space. Identify who will have the left and right side of the bathroom and shared sleeping area. This will allow each person to have his or her own space.

- Cleanup. Make sure you leave the bathroom; shower, sink, and toilet clean for the next person.

- Neatness. Pick up your clothes, accessories, and towels, and put them in a designated area.

- Borrowing. If you have to borrow something, always ask permission first. Return it in the condition in which it was borrowed. If you damage or lose something you borrow, you are responsible for replacement.

- Lights out. Be considerate of others who may go to bed or awaken earlier than you do.

- Quiet time. Discuss with your roommate if you want to increase the volume of music, entertain other guests, or have a party.

Bereavement Etiquette

During your career, you might experience the loss of a co-worker, manager, company executive, a personal family member, or a friend. We often do not know what to do when someone has experienced a loss. It is important to remember that doing or saying something is better than doing nothing at all.

The following are bereavement etiquette strategies for sending condolences:

Phone Calls

Phone calls may be intrusive unless you are close to the co-worker or family. The bereaved do not want the burden of making repeated polite conversation with people on the phone during their loss and healing process.

If you decide to make a phone call, make it short. Ask if you or your organization can do anything to assist the family.

Written Notes

You may decide to send a personal written note or sympathy card to the co-worker who has experienced a loss.

E-mail

E-mail is acceptable to send to a co-worker who has lost a family member or close friend. Although the co-worker may not receive it until they return to work, it shows you were thinking about them during their loss.

Donations

Sending a donation is an option to sending flowers.

- Find out the charities, foundations, or associations to which the family would like you to make a contribution on behalf of the deceased.

- The charity, foundation, and association websites will guide you through the donation procedure, or you can contact them directly for donation information.

How Much Do You Donate?

- The amount you donate depends on your relationship with the person or organization.

- Send a note to the family on company letterhead explaining that a donation has been made. Listing the amount of the donation is optional.

Cultural Sensitivity

Different bereavement customs are practiced by different cultures. To determine the appropriate practice

- Find a website with information.

- Ask for help from those of the same culture.

Follow-up

Depending on cultural practices, follow-up in a few weeks to let the bereaved know you are thinking of them.

If you send flowers, a note or poem may be used upon your good judgment.

Healing After a Loss

For you (the bereaved)

- Ask for help if you need it.

- Express your feelings to others.

- Be aware of your physical needs.

- Learn more about grief.

- Give yourself time to heal.

For co-workers, family, friends, and others who care

- Be a good listener.
- Be available for the bereaved.
- Be patient.
- Let the person cry.
- Provide support.
- Do not say you know how they feel.

Ask How You Can Help

Helping or taking over a task at work might be helpful and appreciated.

Be specific in your offer to help, and follow up with action.

Danger Signs

Observing the following signs may mean the bereaved person needs professional help.

- Depression
- Lack of personal hygiene
- Physical problems
- Sleeping disorders
- Substance abuse
- Substantial weight loss
- Talking about suicide

Bereavement Etiquette for Pets

Pets, for many people, are seen as family members. The death of a pet can affect your life more than the death of a relative or friend. The following are tips to help you and a co-worker, family, or friend through the loss of their pet:

- Sympathy Card. Send a pet sympathy card to a co-worker, family member, or friend who has suffered a pet loss.
- E-mail. Send an e-mail expressing sympathy for the loss of a persons pet.

- Pet cemetery. Contact your local pet cemetery for services they may provide.

- Write a poem. Writing poetry about your pet may be relaxing.

- Scrapbook. Preparing a scrapbook of favorite photos is comforting.

- Distractions. Spending time with family and friends will help distract you from your loss.

Disaster and Tragedy Etiquette

Disasters and tragedies come in all forms and can disrupt the work and life of co-workers, family, and friends. Both are unpredictable, and therefore no one can plan for their prevention.

At work, co-workers are often faced with feelings of "what should I do?" when informed that either of these has touched the life of a fellow employee. Helping others in their time of need is the first step. You don't have to be a friend or know someone personally to offer assistance. Listed, are easy basic tips to follow when providing help for people who have experienced an unfortunate situation.

- Give comfort and support.

- Be a good listener. Listening to those who are suffering is a good prescription for healing.

- Be hands-on. Ask how you can make a difference. Depending on the situation, you might be asked to take over a work assignment, collect donations, prepare flyers, help locate temporary shelter, contact local and out-of-state family members, and others.

Respect People Who Experience a Disaster or Tragedy

- Understand that people need time to grieve their experience.

- Be available if they need a shoulder to lean on.

- Do what you can to help ease their pain.

- Ask others to help if you need assistance.

Professional etiquette helps to create the confidence you need in order to improve your behavior in the workplace, by knowing how to deal with situations both ordinary and exceptional, and by being able to appreciate good etiquette in others.

Etiquette is a key factor in dealing with all customers, whether internal or external and will most certainly have a determining factor in the progress of your career.

Networking: 17 Essential Strategies for the 21st Century

Introduction

Effective networking strategies provide access to knowledge, expertise, and allies to support you both professionally and personally. Networking requires a mission, goals, vision, and a willingness to share valuable information with others. Networking events are places to make plans to reconnect and stay in touch.

Networking is building relationships, helping others and giving advice to anyone who asks. A trusting business relationship will enhance your base of contacts and build a lifetime of rewards.

It's not who you know, it's who knows you!

Strategy 1: Introductions and Marketing Statement ("Elevator Speech")

First Impressions

Make positive first impressions with business associates and colleagues.

Three Tips for Introductions

1. Make eye contact and extend a confident handshake.

2. Eliminate trendy words such as "cool" and "awesome" from your vocabulary in a business environment.

3. Carry company materials that represent your organization, such as pens, Post-it-Notes, or a computer bag. These items are a positive reflection of you and represent your organizational and professional style.

The Proper Handshake

The purpose of a handshake is to establish rapport and positive chemistry between two people. A handshake is a form of non-verbal communication. It is appropriate to shake hands in a business setting. Gender does not determine whether to shake hands or not.

Your handshake communicates:

- Professionalism
- Confidence
- Credibility

When to Stand

It is proper to stand when shaking hands during introductions unless you are seated in an environment such as a restaurant that makes standing difficult. Standing balances the power between you and your contact. The person standing is presumed to have the power.

A firm handshake conveys

- Assurance
- Confidence
- Interest
- Respect

The Name Game

Everyone likes to have his or her name remembered, pronounced, and spelled correctly. Making an effort to remember names strengthens personal and business relationships.

Here are six techniques to help you remember names:

1. Listen carefully to people's names.
2. If you are not sure you heard the person's name correctly, or if you did not understand what the person said, ask them to repeat the name.
3. Repeat the name back to the person for reinforcement and confirmation only if you did not understand.
4. Break the name down into syllables for yourself.

5. Connect the name with something familiar to you.

6. Identify something unique about the person and their name.

Marketing Statement (also known as "Elevator Speech or "Introduction")

Your marketing statement should be something about yourself that engages people in a conversation. Tailor your marketing statement to the event. It should be:

- Planned – Write down what you want to say prior to the event.

- Practiced – Rehearse out loud prior to the event to hear how you sound.

- Succinct – Make sure you pronounce your words clearly.

- Interesting – Use humor to create interest in your introduction.

Example:

Hello, my name is Heather Sunset from San Diego, California. I'm attending the Women's History Month National Training Conference.

Strategy 2: Power Image Tips

Make a power statement – Show You Mean Business!

Dressing appropriately for business in the 21st Century is an essential element of doing business. Never underestimate the power of first impressions.

It takes ten seconds or less for someone to form an impression of you based on what they see.

In business, power and credibility are based on people's perception of you. So position yourself where you want to go professionally; your clothing sends a message about how serious you are. Ask yourself, "What image do I project?" What you wear today could impact your image tomorrow.

Appearances do count

Appearance is based on the following percentages and characteristics.

- Appearance and body language – 55%
- Vocal tone, pacing, and voice inflection – 38%
- Verbal message – 7%

Power Image Career Opportunities

- You never know who is observing your appearance.

- Position your image for promotions.

- Dress for your next position.

- Think about the perception others might have of your non-verbal communication.

- Consider the positive or negative impact your image can have on your career and future.

- Make business decisions.

Strategy 3:
Define Your Networking Goals

Write specific long- and short-term goals.

WHAT are your goals?

Immediate: Three to six months

Short-term: Nine to twelve months

Long-term: One to five years

WHY are these goals important to you?

Have you made the commitment to achieve these goals?

WHO are the people I need to help me?

How can I recruit them? How can they help me?

WHEN can I expect to achieve my goals?

How will I know when I have achieved them?

Strategy 4: Information, Influence, Resources, and Volunteer

Know what you have to offer and what you have to gain.

Information

Seek information relative to your job search or business needs. Use networking website resources to assist you in your search.

Influence

- Define a strategy to meet and network with new people.

- Position yourself to have access to key people.

- Identify people who have the ability to connect you to what you need to achieve your goal.

Resources

- Know where to go. Ask questions if you need assistance.

- Make reasonable requests from your network.

- Do not ask for more than a person can afford to give.

- Be considerate of your contact's position and yours.

Volunteer

- Volunteer for career and business projects.

- Network while helping a personal, professional, or business cause.

- Volunteer work gives you the opportunity to get involved and show your skills to potential future business contacts.

Strategy 5:
Effective Business Card Exchange

Effective business card exchange occurs when your contact can become a resource for you or others you know.

Exchanging business cards with someone does not constitute a networking relationship. Challenge yourself not to give out your cards, until you have uncovered a reason for exchanging names and phone numbers.

Lead your conversation in a direction that it may be beneficial for you and your contact to exchange business cards beyond the event purpose.

Business Card Exchange Tips

Read your contact's business card carefully and ask questions about information on the card. Asking questions shows interest in your contact and is a great way to start a conversation.

- Bring enough business cards.

- Date the card. Put the date on the front right corner of the card; put the event or occasion and additional notes on the back of the card as a reference.

- Devise a personal system for exchanging your cards with your contacts.

- Ask about unique spellings of an individual or a company name.

- Ask about initials, degrees, and certifications.

- Ask about industries of which you have little or no knowledge.

- Clarify whether the person works for a company or is an entrepreneur.

Networking Signature Tools

- Custom name badge – Invest in a custom-prepared name badge. Put your name, company name, or field of interest on the name badge. Wear your name badge on the right side, this will ensure your name is clearly seen when you shake hands.

- Quality pen and pencil set – Purchase a quality brand pen and pencil set, or have others give them to you as a gift on your birthday or special occasion. Engraving your name is a professional touch.

- Quality business cards – Invest in quality business cards. Another alternative is to purchase a business card kit from a stationary supply store and make them on your computer.

- Leather writing portfolio – Always be prepared to take notes. Select a leather writing portfolio that will accommodate a notepad and one that has a pocket to store your business cards.

Strategy 6:
Four Tools for Contact Management

Make time to keep in touch.

After a networking event, sort through business cards to determine which ones you need, and follow up with those contacts within three business days.

Develop a system to manage your contacts easily using these four tools:

- Invest in contact management software.

- Use a three-ring notebook with plastic pages for inserting business cards.

- Purchase a pocket contact software system and have your information with you.

- Use a business card filing system on your desk.

Strategy 7:
Seven Keys to Conversation

Small conversations are an effective way to learn about each other.

Use your experiences and environment to create conversations about business, career, sports, lifestyle, and other topics that will help others feel comfortable with you.

1. Listen to world news or read the newspaper daily.

2. Avoid sensitive topics such as sex, religion, and politics unless you are attending a function involving those topics.

3. Read newsletters, professional journals, and magazines.

4. Take notes about important information for your networking goals.

5. Use humor in good taste and avoid sexist and racial comments.

6. Listen actively.

7. Say YES to new business and professional opportunities!

Strategy 8: Engage Your Connection

Make a commitment to learn public speaking skills. Listen and observe speaking styles of others you admire and want to incorporate with your personal style.

The letters in the word "engage" will help you remember the process of engaging your connection in a conversation.

- Eye – Establish and maintain good eye contact.

- Nod – Nod to encourage communication.

- Greet – Greet people with a friendly smile, hello, and handshake.

- Attention – Focus your attention on what is being said.

- Gesturing – Gesturing your hands when you talk enhances your message.

- Ease – Be at ease and comfortable with your connection.

Strategy 9: Close the Conversation

Six Strategies

Use closing statements that will help you transition to your next contact. When you leave gracefully, you leave the door open to reconnect at another time.

1. I want to meet the host.

2. I want to meet the speaker.

3. I promised to meet with a few colleagues before they leave.

4. I'm going to meet new potential clients.

5. I want to say hello to an existing client.

6. I do not want to take your networking time.

L.E.A.V.E. Technique

- **L**et go of your contact after five minutes to work the event.

- **E**xplain why you are there and find out why your connection is there.

- **A**ct on your planned agenda.

- **V**isualize your next move.

- **E**xit gracefully after shaking hands.

Strategy 10:
Seven Magnificent Listening Tips

1. Focus on the speaker.

2. Listen to understand from the speaker's perspective.

3. Maintain good eye contact.

4. Ask questions and provide feedback that demonstrates your interest.

5. Observe others' body language.

6. Identify and acknowledge mutual interests.

7. Keep an open mind and take mental and written notes. When you identify you have something to offer, the next step is to exchange business cards, ideas, resources, and referrals. Show your competence in what you say and do. Always respect confidentiality and support the success of your contact.

Strategy 11: Working the Room

Plan Your Presence

- Be a good listener and encourage others to share information. When people talk about themselves you find out about them and their business.

- Work the room with a goal in mind.

- Do not spend the entire time with one person.

- Limit the amount of time you spend with people you know.

- Be kind to everyone!

- Do not judge others based on physical appearances and disabilities – be open to all people.

- Use good business judgment.

- Ask the right questions and gather valuable information.

- Focus on what you have in common – the event.

- Be aware of body language. When two people are face-to-face, they usually do not want to be interrupted. If they are standing side-by-side, it is more likely you are welcomed to join their conversation.

- Ask permission to join a group of three or more. Never interrupt or change the subject they are discussing; wait for a break in the conversation.

- Limit your comments to three to five minutes and invite feedback from others.

Strategy 12: Ten Trust Ingredients

Teach Your Contacts about Your Character

Contacts must see you in action to observe your behavior or hear favorable comments about you from others. If you make a commitment to do something, follow it through.

Here are ten guidelines to help teach contacts about your character.

1. Be reliable.

2. Meet deadlines and commitments.

3. Create win-win-win solutions.

4. Treat everyone with respect.

5. Speak positively about all people.

6. Collaborate with others rather than compete.

7. Correct mistakes and apologize.

8. Go the extra mile – do more than what is expected.

9. Respect other people's time and privacy.

10. Compensate for failures – offer to volunteer your services or help someone who might need your assistance.

Strategy 13:
Power Etiquette and Manners

Good manners can open doors that money, position, and power cannot.

Power Etiquette

How you relate to others is what etiquette is all about. Your attitude is a personality trait developed throughout your life. Understand the power of your attitude; it impacts everything you do.

Signs of Your Attitude

- Your body language.
- How you take care of yourself.
- How you complete your assignments.
- Your attention to detail.

Good Manners in Business

Good manners can open doors that money, position, and power cannot.

- Respect the organization's culture.
- Treat rank with respect.
- Respect others and their privacy.
- Be courteous to others.

Cell Phones and Pagers

Use good business judgment. Turn off cell phones and pagers prior to:

- Networking functions.
- All business-related functions.

Use the vibration option to alert you of messages.

- Do not answer your phone call or look at your pager in the presence of others.
- When you look at your cell phone or pager, your contact will think you need to leave the conversation.
- Gracefully exit before leaving to respond to an alert.

Strategy 14: Follow Up

Visibility is valuable.

R.E.A.C.H Technique

Effective follow-up is the most important step in the networking process. Often, people invest their time, energy, and money to attend functions and make contacts, but spend little or no time in building relationships with others. Following up and keeping in touch are essential for successful networking.

- Relationships – Build relationships with networking contacts.

- Engage – Engage contacts in a meaningful conversation.

- Action – Take action based on your outcome.

- Contact – Contact referrals instrumental to your success.

- How – Ask how you can become a resource for others.

Strategy 15: Network at Work

*Networking in the 21st century is more important
for your career than ever before.*

Win Inside

No matter where you work—a government agency, a corporation, a non-profit organization, or an association—networking is more important to your career than ever before.

Traditional career paths are rapidly changing. People must rely on their own ability to build networks at work and manage their careers. "Social networking" is a preferred alternative to traditional organizational charts and everyday business transactions.

A network of contacts—both inside and outside of an organization— is the most important thing a professional can do for their career. To get a promotion, spend time networking.

It's Not Who You Know...It's Who Knows You!

Why Network at Work?

Change – Use your network to stay informed about organizational change.

Bottom Line – Your job depends on the success of the organization.

Venture – Step out into non-traditional career opportunities.

Collaboration – Increase teamwork with other people and departments.

Expand Your Knowledge – Create a network of people with different interests and expertise.

Benefits

- Increase visibility. New opportunities will find you.
- Accountability and responsibility. Manage your "own" career.
- Options. Always keep your career and business options open.

Transitional Skills

- Determine a strategy to showcase your skills, abilities, and interest to others.

Networking Thoughts

- What resources do you have to help others?
- What can you offer others in your networking relationship?

Strategy 16:
Networking Organizations

Networking with people will bring you a world of opportunities.

- Visibility is valuable. Make the most of your time.
- Arrive early, stay late, and meet the movers and shakers.
- Make conversation about your career, business goals, or other objectives.
- Become a resource for others.

Strategy 17:
Networking As a Way of Life

Networking has a beginning but no end.

Networking will bring you personal and professional success. Make the most of your time; be determined, patient, and visible.

Practice conversations with people in familiar and uncommon places. Asking questions is a sign of a good listener and will help you establish rapport and build relationships. Networking has a beginning and no end.

Developing Your Network:
The Smartest Business Decision

"Networking is building relationships, helping others,
and giving advice to anyone who asks." —Patricia Dorch

Implementing these clear strategies will impact your success both professionally and personally. Listed are tips to help you become more successful at networking.

- Names – Remember people's names.

- Eye – Eye contact is important.

- Talk – Talk, but also listen to what is being said.

- Write – Write follow-up notes on a regular basis.

- Open – Be open and ask questions.

- Resource – Become a resource for others.

- Knowledge – Knowledge is the ability to control your destiny.

Summary:
Six Figure Career Advice for Everyone

Whether you're new to the workforce or you've been in it for years, you can benefit from the useful advice you've just read in these pages! Refer back to Patricia Dorch's Six Figure Career Coaching Advice: The Ultimate Guide to Achieving Success often to help you polish your image and upgrade your career by:

- Taking proactive steps on a consistent basis to be ready for interviews and career advancement

- Using body language - and what mannerisms to avoid - in a job interview or when interacting with co-workers

- Asking the right questions in your first interview to gain a second interview

- Using power business tools and accessories to get you noticed

- Never underestimating the power of a "business casual" meeting

- Utilizing the "new networking" of the 21st Century to leverage career opportunities

Remember, perfecting your business image requires an ongoing process, but it's worth the work – you'll be ready to take advantage of career-building opportunities. And once your career is on track, you'll more than likely see improvement in other parts of your life to.

"When you help to develop people,
you empower them to improve as individuals"

—Patricia Dorch, M.S.

About the Author

PATRICIA DORCH, President and CEO of EXECU DRESS, is a renowned business image, etiquette, and career expert. She advises major corporations, associations, government entities, educational institutions, and others on proper business and business casual image dress guidelines and self-improvement skills – all areas that can make a huge difference in an employee's career and company's success. Patricia Dorch is a dynamic speaker and trainer who specialize in professional development and personal success.

www.ingramcontent.com/pod-product-compliance
Lightning Source LLC
Chambersburg PA
CBHW060623200326
41521CB00007B/865